Following The Great Spirit

Michael B. Davie

Manor House Publishing Inc.

1

National Library of Canada Cataloguing in Publication Data:

Davie, Michael B., 1954-
Following The Great Spirit
Exploring Aboriginal Belief Systems

1st ed.
Includes bibliographical references and notes.

ISBN: 978-0-9685803-8-7

1. Indigenous peoples – Religion.
I. Title.

GN470.D38 2001   306'.08   C2001-903928-X

Published November 15, 2001
by Manor House Publishing: **(905) 648-2193**

First Edition.
Cover Design: Michael B. Davie.
Technical assistance/realization: Richard Kosydar.

By Michael B. Davie:

The Late Man MH
A Novel

Following The Great Spirit MH
Exploring Native Indian Belief Systems

Political Losers MH
The Lessons Of Failure

Distant Voices MH
Canadian Politics On the Outside Looking In

Canada Decentralized MH
Can Our Nation Survive?

Quebec and Section 33 MH
Why The Notwithstanding Clause Must Not Stand

Inside the Witches' Coven MH
Exploring Wiccan Rituals

Enterprise 2000 MH
Hamilton, Halton, Niagara Embrace the Millennium

Success Stories BR

Business Achievement in Greater Hamilton
Hamilton: It's Happening* BR
Celebrating Hamilton's Sesquicentennial

MH = Published by Manor House Publishing.
BR = Published by BRaSH Publishing
* = With co-author Sherry Sleightholm

3

Belated Credit for Past Work:

Please note: Regarding the books Canada Decentralized, Quebec And Section 33 and Inside The Witches' Coven, all by Michael B. Davie, and Mystical Poetry by Deborah Morrison, Davie should have received credit for the cover design on all four books.

Regarding the book Enterprise 2000: Greater Hamilton, Halton and Niagara embrace the New Millennium, author Michael B. Davie should have received credit for the concept and design of the book's cover.

The cover depicted a limitless horizon with, in the foreground, a New Year's baby seated at a computer with the image repeated endlessly on the computer screen.

Davie also originated the back cover concept of the author leaning on the computer monitor showing the baby image, again repeated endlessly.

Photographer Paul Sparrow should have received credit for bringing these images to realization through his skilful photographic and computer montage work.

– Manor House Publishing Inc.

For
Philippa

Acknowledgements

This book would not have been possible without the thoughtful, analytical works of anthropologists more seasoned and insightful than I.

I am grateful for the expert teachings of the anthropologists and Native culture experts I've cited in this book and for the patient distilling of knowledge by my McMaster University professors who helped me to earn honours degrees in Political Science.

As well, I appreciate the assistance extended by many conscientious people, too numerous to mention, in bringing this book to fruition.

My thanks, as always, to my wife Philippa for her constant encouragement and faith in the validity of my misadventures.

- **Michael B. Davie**.

About the author

One of Canada's most intriguing writers, Michael B. Davie is the author of such critically acclaimed business books as Enterprise 2000 and Success Stories.

The award-winning writer is also the author of nationally important books Political Losers, Canada Decentralized and Quebec & Section 33: Why the Notwithstanding Clause Must Not Stand. He also wrote The Late Man, his 10th book and first novel.

Michael B. Davie is also a journalist with The Toronto Star, Canada's largest newspaper, reaching millions of readers daily.

The author has won dozens of awards for outstanding journalism. His work has also appeared in such major Canadian newspapers as the Halifax Chronicle-Herald, Montreal Gazette, Calgary Herald, Winnipeg Free Press, Edmonton Journal and Vancouver Sun.

Prior to The Star, he was an editor with The Globe and Mail, Canada's national newspaper with coast-to-coast readership.

Previous to The Globe, he spent 17 years with The Hamilton Spectator, where he won 28 journalism awards.

Prior to joining The Spectator, he spent five years with other publications, including the daily Welland Tribune where he was a reporter, columnist and editor.

He also served two years as regional news editor for one of Ontario's largest chains of community newspapers.

Born in Hamilton in 1954, Michael B. Davie's interest in writing began in early childhood. As a preschool child, he became withdrawn and was in a state of shock after his parents decided to divorce. During a visit to a community centre, the child opened the door to a room to find child psychologists had been studying him through two-way mirrors.

The young child then began closely observing other children and adults, studying their interaction and watching their stories unfold. By the late 1960s and into the 1970s, while in his teens, he was a contributing writer to counter culture publications.

He turned professional in the mid-1970s as Editor of The Phoenix serving Mohawk College of Applied Arts & Technology where he earned a Broadcast Journalism diploma.

He also holds a Niagara College Print Journalism diploma and degrees in Political Science from McMaster University where he was repeatedly named to the Deans' Honour List and won the Political Science Prize for outstanding academic achievement.

Michael B. Davie currently resides in Ancaster with his wife Philippa and their children Donovan, Sarah and Ryan.

Contents

Manor House Publishing Inc.
(905) 648-2193.

Opening Notes

Following the Great Spirit examines some of the cultural values and spiritual mindset of North American Indians and other aboriginal peoples in crisis situations and times of great change.

Within this context, we take a look at the connection of aboriginal people to the land, to the natural world to ancient rituals and long established traditions.

And we'll explore their reliance – much like the rest of us – on turning to powers greater than themselves in times of upheaval.

We begin with a look at the Ghost Dance, a phenomena that sprang forth when North American Indians were displaced from hunting grounds, dispossessed of lands and in some cases assimilated to accommodate encroaching white settlements in the latter half of the 1800s.

During this time, much of the Native population had been wiped out by such White man's diseases as small pox and the buffalo had been hunted nearly to extinction.

And so the Indians turned to the Ghost Dance for salvation.

We'll examine the Ghost Dance as a somewhat-utopian spiritual belief system that helped the dispossessed Cherokee, Sioux, Paiute, Klamath and Plains Indians in the U.S., and Dakota Indians in Canada, cope with their sudden displacement, alienation and rapidly growing sense of despair.

As we'll learn, the Ghost Dance comforted the oppressed Indians as performing the dance could, supposedly, bring about the return of lost people and game in abundance, with Indians displacing whites to regain their former relationship with the land.

This spiritual dance promised the return of dead Indians and game in a new age of abundance, with the Indians being very much in control of their collective destiny.

In examining the Ghost Dance, we'll also compare it to cargo cults, another manifestation of an oppressed people's spiritual need to find a utopian solution to an all-encompassing threat against the continued existence of their culture.

The cargo cults of New Guinea and Melanesia also allowed practitioners to use religious principles to help their followers cope with a crisis that has thwarted their efforts to have a more satisfying culture.

Cargo cults offer a revivalistic appeal, as the cult followers believe through their prophecies and myth dreams that they will be reunited with long-dead ancestors in a golden age of prosperity.

These cults also put the Indians in charge while the White men are eradicated – but leave their possessions (cargo) behind for the Natives to enjoy.

Indeed, the cargo cults offer a heady mixture of salvation and revenge and prosperity.

We'll also explore the rare, exulted status Indians enjoyed through the boom times of the fur trade.

To a significant degree, the extent to which Euro-Canadians depended on Indians, for survival, furs or food and provisions, strongly influenced the degree to which Indians were valued in the emerging Canadian society and the extent to which their personal freedoms, culture and autonomy could be sustained.

The fur trade had a profound impact on the independence of Indians and their ability to be masters of their own destiny.

Our chapter on the fur trade will argue that in sharp contrast to dispossessed east coastal Indians, those Indians engaged in the fur trade were accorded a far higher status and effective recognition of autonomy by white society due to the dependence of Euro-Canadian fur traders on Indians to trap and supply furs, and provisions.

However, this temporary prosperity was not without its cultural and spiritual costs. As we'll learn, the Indians lost a great deal when the fur trade boom times came to an end.

To get a sense of how badly things can go

awry when Indians lose their value in White society, we have a review of Hugh Brody's excellent maps And Dreams.

Brody spent a great deal of time with the Beaver tribe of British Columbia as an expert participant observer, and he reported at length on various government efforts to help the Beaver – while disregarding their native culture.

Brody invariably found the consistent government assumption was that the Beaver were a dying people – who just happened to be taking thousands of years to die out.

Finally, we'll explore the Gisaro ceremony and the way it reveals a great deal about the cultural and societal values of the Kaluli people of the Bosavi region of the great Papuan Plateau on the island of New Guinea.

As we'll discover, with its central characteristics of reciprocity and emotional release, Gisaro transcends the limitations of a ceremonial dance to embody the deepest, most personal experiences of the audience.

Gisaro is very much both a spiritual and emotional experience in which members of the audience are made to cry and then burn the dancers for making them weep.

In the Gisaro chapter, we'll examine these aspects of this cultural phenomenon, as presented by Edward L. Schieffelin in his book The Sorrow of the Lonely and the Burning of the Dancers.

Schieffelin, whose field work included two years - 1966-1968 - among the Kaluli, remarked on the powerful socializing role of Gisaro, observing that Gisaro is the "most elaborate and characteristic ceremony of this type."

And we'll explore how Gisaro plays a key role in illustrating and perpetuating the societal value system of the Kaluli.

We have a fascinating journey ahead of us. And our journey begins now.

- **Michael B. Davie.**

Following The Great Spirit

Michael B. Davie

"… interesting and well referenced… good, clear conclusions…well situated in anthropological literature on the cults of despair."

- McMaster University Anthropology Professor Victor Gulewitsch critiquing Dances With Ghosts by Michael B. Davie.

Chapter One

Dances With Ghosts

Exploring the North American Indians' Ghost
Dance as a cultural phenomenon of nativism
and revivalism

The Ghost Dance arose during a period of
great cultural and social upheaval in the latter half of
the 1800s, when many North American aboriginal
groups were displaced from hunting grounds to
accommodate encroaching white settlements.

These groups were also dispossessed of their
lands and left struggling to resist cultural encapsulation by the European-derived culture spreading across
North America.

The Ghost Dance arose as an expression of nativism and revivalism by Plains Indians and other aboriginal peoples who turned to a new, somewhat-utopian spiritual belief system to help them cope with displacement, alienation and despair.

This chapter will compare and contrast the Ghost Dance to cargo cults, another manifestation of an oppressed people's spiritual need to find a utopian solution to an all-encompassing threat against the continued existence of their culture.

A combination of dire circumstances placed the Indian peoples of North America in a very precarious position in the latter half of the 1800s.

Small pox and other European diseases had virtually wiped out two-thirds or more of many tribes.

As well, the buffalo, a major source of food for Plains Indians, had almost been rendered extinct through over-hunting by largely non-native hunters. (Thornton, 1987: pp. 103-125).

And, the Cherokee and many other aboriginal

groups were forcibly dispossessed of hunting lands and relocated to marginal areas to make room for agrarian colonization by the rapidly expanding society of white settlers. (Thornton, 1987: pp. 103-125).

The severity of the Indians' collective plight, and their seeming inability to push away the intruding European presence that was clearly dominating them, resulted in a religious, spiritual response, the Ghost Dance.

The Ghost Dance served to comfort the oppressed Indians by offering the assurance that practicing the dance would bring the return of lost people and game in abundance, with Indians displacing whites to regain their former relationship with the land.

Anthony Wallace asserts that the Ghost Dance was rivivalistic as it had the purpose of reviving and restoring a lost way of life, to the extent that even dead Indians, animals and fish would come back to life in a reborn age of abundance with Indians very clearly in control. (Wallace, 1972: pp. 340-343).

Wallace also describes the Ghost Dance as nativistic because it also held the intent of purging the lands of white European-American settlers to free the Indians from domination by white people. (Wallace, 1972: pp. 340-343).

With its features of nativism and revivalism, the Ghost Dance formed the core of a wider revitalization movement to breathe new life and hope into an impoverished and oppressed culture. (Wallace, 1972: pp. 340-343).

Wallace also finds similarities between the Ghost Dance and another revitalization movement; the cargo cults of New Guinea and Melanesia.

Both the Ghost Dance and cargo cults practitioners use religious principles to help their followers cope with a crisis that has thwarted their efforts to have a more satisfying culture. (Wallace, 1972: pp. 340-343).

As in the Ghost Dance, the cargo cults are religions of the oppressed.

Cargo cults offer a revivalistic appeal, as the cult followers believe through their prophecies and myth dreams that they will be reunited with long-dead ancestors in a golden age of prosperity. (Wallace, 1972: pp. 340-343).

Cargo cults can also be seen as nativistic, as the cults also call for the presence of white people to be removed. (Wallace, 1972: p. 342).

However, cargo cults differ from the Ghost

Dance in one important area: The cargo cults are somewhat acculturalistic as they conveniently predict that when the whites vanish, they will leave behind all of their various material possessions – or cargo – for native use.

Such a 'heritage' would thereby lead to the natives' adoption and expansion of alien ways and technology at the probable risk of losing some native ways.

Describing the more extreme forms of cargo cults which feature an apocalypse of white people, Peter Worsley notes the cargo cults offer a heady mixture of salvation and revenge and prosperity.

Worsley suggests that it's this promise of better times ahead that serves to lure many into the cult and turns an oppressed people into believers of a cult-offered salvation.

As Worsley observes:

"...these cults all advance the same central theme: the world is about to end in a terrible cataclysm. Thereafter God, the ancestors, or some local hero will appear to inaugurate a blissful paradise on earth. Death, old age, illness and evil will be unknown. The riches of the white man will accrue to the Melanesians." (Worsley, 1959: p. 346).

In contrast, the Ghost dance seeks a total

rejection of both white people and their culture (with the exception of previously adopted technologies, horses and goods) while restoring native customs and ways.

Instead of embracing white culture, the Ghost Dance strives to more fully restore the aboriginal culture which would then cease to fall under the influence of the formerly dominant, alien white culture. (Wallace, 1972: p. 342).

Despite this significant difference, both the Ghost Dance and cargo cults share a greater number of similarities, already outlined, and both fall well within the bounds of revitalization movements. (Wallace, 1972: p. 342).

Indeed, some later, more extreme versions of the Ghost Dance also called for an apocalypse of white people. (Wallace, 1972: p. 342).

The concept of apocalypse gives comfort to followers of religions of the oppressed because it flows from a set of ultimately-rewarding assumptions, including: the belief that the present is a pivotal point in history in which great change will occur.

Other assumptions include; that evil enemies who now dominate will soon be wiped out; and that the formerly-dominated people will rise from the wreckage to enjoy lives of abundance and happiness, free from former oppressors who would no longer exist. (Cummins, Green and Verhulst, 1972: p. 255).

I. M. Lewis, a noted anthropology professor at the London School of Economics and Political Science, has examined this phenomena and asserts that the spiritual power of "religions of the oppressed" often arises through the emergence of leaders who:

"...in response to new stimuli and pressures announce messianic revelations and inaugurate spiritually inspired religions with a new and wider appeal." (Lewis, 1986: p. 46).

For the message of a spiritual leader or prophet to gain acceptance from the masses, a set of pre-revivalist movement conditions are usually present.

The set of phases leading to a Ghost Dance is described by Wallace as including: a steady, calm state in which the society is somewhat at ease with itself and is not interested in radical change. (Wallace, 1972: p. 341).

Another phase is a period of increased stress in which "depression, famine, conquest by an outside, alien society, and acculturation pressures... lead to the awareness of a growing discrepancy between life as it is and life as it could be," notes Wallace. (Wallace, 1972: p. 341).

All of this, according to Wallace, results in a population in duress; And this in turn leads to a period of cultural distortion in which people find their intolerable situation cannot effectively be resolved through conventional beliefs or ways.

And so, in desperation, they then turn to idiosyncratic, deviant or somewhat radical solutions. (Wallace, 1972: p. 341).

A movement phase follows in which a prophet emerges from the society's severe state of unrest with a soothing vision, allegedly sent from supernatural beings, which offers salvation and a better, even utopian, life to those who carry out the vision's instructions. (Wallace, 1972: p. 341).

Next, the prophet preaches his revelation to the people, attracting mass followers and social organization while converting disbelievers to the cause. (Wallace, 1972: p. 341).

And, finally, the prophecy may eventually become an institutionalized part of the society. (Wallace, 1972: p. 341).

Given the dire conditions Indians found themselves in, it is not altogether surprising that some of the oppressed Plains Indians went through the phases just described. (Wallace, 1972: p. 341).

Nor is it surprising that they turned to a prophet in their midst, and embraced the Ghost Dance as their way to escape oppression and achieve a better life. (Wallace, 1972: p. 341).

In essence, a desperate people were embracing the Ghost Dance – tailor made to turn around the forces of oppression.

As Russell Thornton observes:
"In response to severe demographic losses... social and cultural collapse, many western American Indian tribes... sought to re-establish former societies, cultures, even populations. To do so, they created two new religions, or revitalization movements - one around 1870, the other around 1890 - which were deliberate group efforts to reaffirm or recreate established ways of the past. Prophesied in both was a return... of American Indian dead through the performance of prescribed ceremonial dances. Hence the religious movements came to be known as Ghost Dances." (Thornton, 1987: p. 134).

Alice Kehoe notes that the Ghost Dance originated in 1870 among the Paiute of Nevada. Devastated by small pox epidemics, the Walker River

Paiute turned to band leader Wodziwob – also known as Fish Lake Joe – who led them in his own version of the dance. (Kehoe, 1992: p. 328).

The Wodziwob-Paiute Ghost Dance involved the painting of faces and dancing in a circle, round dances, along with trances and the dancers' expressed visions of a restoration of the lost buffalo herds. Wodziwob's Ghost Dance featured a return of the dead to the land of the living. (Kehoe, 1992: p. 328).

The formerly dead were to arrive in Nevada aboard a train from the east. (Kehoe, 1992: p. 328).

Although Wodziwob's Ghost Dance and vision of restored game were followed by a drought and no restoration of lost game or Indian ancestors, the Ghost Dance religion still spread throughout Nevada and into California. (Kehoe, 1992: p. 328).

It also spread as far north as Oregon where it rapidly came to be adopted by other tribes who added their own variations to the dance itself. (Kehoe, 1992: p. 328).

The Klamath of Oregon practiced Ghost Dances from 1870 to 1873 when the ritual was suppressed by Indian agents of the American government who did not fully understand the ritual and were deeply distrustful of its practitioners and their aims. (Kehoe, 1992: p. 328).

Describing this early manifestation of the Ghost Dance, Leslie Spier observes:

"The Klamath thesis was the familiar one that the dead would return if the living danced in a prescribed fashion. Not only the people of the land of the dead, the Nolinskankni, but animals, fish, and food of every description would appear on earth again. The ghosts appeared to visionaries who danced themselves into a trance state, instructed them in the procedure of the dance and gave them songs for it." (Spier, 1927: p. 47).

Recounting details relating to preparation for the Ghost Dance, Spier provides this illustrative passage:

"Dress was stripped away... Both sexes wore only the fringed skirts of sagebrush, the garb of those long dead... Only the face was painted; commonly in short lines marked diagonally inward down the cheeks and on the chin in many colours together. Such painting was dreamed; they saw the ghost painted in this fashion..." (Spier, 1927: p. 48).

Of the Ghost Dance itself, Spier describes in detail an intricate ritual which began with Klamath participants avoiding sleep for many hours. (Spier, 1927: p. 49).

This was in accordance with their professed belief that they would turn to stone if they gave in to sleep during the lengthy dance which began with the Klamath clasping hands and forming a circle ringed by small fires. (Spier, 1927: p. 49).

Spier then adds:
"At the centre of the circle was a striped pole; as each song was begun, the pole swayed to jangle cowbells tied to the top. As they danced, singing, some would topple unconscious in their tracks; then they dreamed songs given by the ghosts. They were carried to the centre and laid in a row while the dance went on without interruption. There were several men called dodeuks, dreamers or prophets, who tended them in their trance... They sprinkled the recumbent forms with branches of white sage dipped in water, and when they revived, led them back to the circle so that they could immediately sing the songs they had dreamed." (Spier, 1927: p. 49).

In 1890, another Ghost Dance vision was expressed by another Nevada Paiute prophet, Wovoka, who was a child of 10 when Wodziwob's vision first generated excitement among the Nevada tribes.

Wovoka's Ghost Dance of 1890 was also partly in response to the dispossession of huge tracts of land lost to settlement.

And it was partly in response to the efforts of some Indian agents of the American government to assimilate – if not disintegrate - aboriginal cultures, in their zeal to take over lands.

Not surprisingly, all of this served to further alienate the Indians.

As Janet McDonnell notes:

"They demanded that the Indians adopt white ways and move into the twentieth century along with the rest of American society, even though the Indians already had their own highly developed culture and value system. The Indians had no concept of permanent ownership and title to land and did not place the same importance on money..." (McDonnell, 1991: p. 124).

The Wovoka Ghost Dance, arriving 20 years after the first known Ghost Dances occurred, also in Nevada, was to have even more dramatic rates of participation and generate more excitement than the original.

In the two-decade period leading up to Wovoka's Ghost Dance, the unacceptable conditions the Indians found themselves in had not improved. (Murphy, 1979: p. 214).

In many ways, white domination had increased with new sets of regulations for the white-controlled Indian reserves. (Murphy, 1979: p. 214).

The severity of these conditions provided a fertile breeding ground for a new Ghost Dance religion which would assure the troubled Indians that their culture and way of life were noble and worth keeping; that only the domination of an evil, alien presence was keeping them from fulfilling a greater destiny; that this situation would soon be corrected as the white presence would be wiped out; and dead Indians would soon rejoin the living in a new golden age. (Murphy, 1979: p. 214).

Commenting on the Indians' dismal conditions and the rise of the Wovoka Ghost Dance, Robert Murphy observes:

"The native peoples of the American West had been mostly subjugated and confined to reservations by the 1870s; their entire economic base had collapsed with the destruction of the buffalo herds and the occupation of their lands by the whites; their political systems had been smashed and outside coercive authority imposed on them; and their religions seemed largely irrelevant to their new way of life. In this atmosphere of total defeat and numbing discouragement, the preachings of a Nevada Paiute shaman named Jack Wovoka offered hope, spreading rapidly across the Rocky Mountains and the Great Plains." (Murphy, 1979: p. 214).

The Ghost Dance also made its way into Canada where Plains Indians had also experienced the loss of the buffalo.

However, the Plains Indians here had generally encountered a less hostile federal government presence and the Ghost Dance was slower to catch on. (McMillan, 1988: pp. 145-146).

In fact, the dance did not spread very far in Canada. As Alan McMillan observes:

"The late religious cults which swept the American Plains were largely ignored in Canada. In their demoralized state, American Plains natives welcomed such messianic movements as the Ghost Dance... In Canada, the Ghost Dance religion was adopted by only small numbers of Dakota in Saskatchewan, and then without the militaristic interpretation of their American Kin." (McMillan, 1988: pp. 145-146).

James Mooney, a nineteenth-century ethnologist who began studying the Wovoka Ghost Dance shortly after it first appeared, conducted an interview with Wovoka in 1892 to gain further insight into this version of the dance and the tragic slaughter of Sioux Indians, which followed its rapid spread. (Mooney, 1896: p. 15).

In a report to the American government, Mooney advised that Wovoka had appeared honest and open during the interview. (Mooney, 1896: p. 15).

For his part, Wovoka denied rumours that he was a reincarnation of Christ although he did assert that he was a prophet who had received the Ghost Dance vision while suffering from a severe fever. (Mooney, 1896: p. 15).

Mooney also advised that the Ghost Dance was a peaceful phenomenon because although it preached the coming return of Indian dead and the vanishing of whites, nothing in its doctrine advocated the forceful expulsion of whites. (Mooney, 1896: p. 15).

Mooney reported that the Ghost Dance had a high moral code of non-violence and merely expressed a belief that white people "will be left behind with the other things of the earth that have served their temporary purpose, or else will cease entirely to exist." (Mooney, 1896: p. 19).

However, Mooney also observed that Wovoka's Ghost Dance became subjected to gross misinterpretations and outright distortions of meaning as it spread across the United States. (Mooney, 1896: p. 19-35).

The Sioux of the Dakotas, embittered by land expropriations and suffering food shortages due to numerous sharp reductions in government-provided rations, gave the Ghost Dance its harshest interpretation, calling for a violent end to white people. (Mooney, 1896: p. 19-35).

So caught up were they in the Ghost Dance culture, the Sioux also created specially-painted Ghost Shirts which were believed by some to be blessed by spirits to make them bullet-proof. (Mooney, 1896: p. 19-35).

As Reginald and Gladys Laubin would later observe of the Ghost Shirt:

> "The early antagonism shown... to the new dance and the fact that the government had now sent up troop reinforcements to

alleviate the settlers' fears led to the adoption of the Ghost Shirt as the most peculiar property in the Sioux Ghost Dance. The Ghost Shirt... was cut in the style of the old-time war shirt and sewed with sinew...The fringe and portions of the shirt were painted with sacred paint obtained from the Messiah... The Sioux were the only Indians to make the garments of cotton and to proclaim them bullet-proof. The Sioux medicine men started this belief in order to allay fears due to the presence of soldiers." (Laubin and Laubin, 1976: p. 60).

Unfortunately for the Sioux, any belief that the Ghost Shirts were bullet-proof was soon proven to be completely unwarranted.

As tensions mounted over the Ghost Dance, the soldiers observing it opened fire with tragic results. (Murphy, 1979: p. 214).

As Murphy observes:
"It was a thoroughly non-violent form of protest, but the whites were contemptuous of Indian religion and suspicious of any gatherings of large numbers of people. In this atmosphere, the U.S. Army attacked a Ghost Dance meeting at Wounded Knee on the Sioux reservation in South Dakota on December 29, 1890, killing over 200 children, women, and men, and even managing to hit a few of their

own in the crossfire." (Murphy, 1979: p. 214).

It is difficult to comprehend how, even given their state of deep despair, the Sioux were able to believe that cotton clothing could repel bullets.

However, the late, Pulitzer Prize-winning social theorist, anthropologist, sociologist and psychologist Ernest Becker has shared some insightful thoughts on underlying motivations for any given culture embracing, beyond apparent reason, an unusual yet heroic mythology of salvation. (Becker, 1962: p. x).

Becker suggest that such a seemingly bizarre action may stem from man's:
> "...basic animal fears... his deep and indelible anxieties about his own impotence and death, and his fear of being overwhelmed and sucked up into the world and into others." (Becker, 1962: p. x).

As Becker notes in an observation that could well apply to the Sioux:
> "Whole societies have been able to persist with central beliefs that bore little relation to reality. About the only time a culture has to pay has been in encounters with conquerors superior in numbers, weapons, and immunity to disease." (Becker, 1962: p. 128).

Finally, in a direct reference to the Sioux and the Ghost Shirt, Becker describes the result that can occur when a movement based purely on myth and wishes for a better life is finally exposed.

As Becker notes:
"...anthropology has taught us that when a culture comes up against reality on certain critical points of its perceptions, and proves them fictional, then that culture is indeed eliminated by what we would call 'natural selection'. When the Plains Indians hurled themselves against White man's bullets thinking themselves immune due to the protection of Guardian Spirits in the invisible world, they were mowed down pitilessly." (Becker, 1962: pp. 127-128).

Although the Ghost Dance has survived as a sometimes-practiced cultural event, it has ceased to exist in the extreme, distorted and discredited form used by the Sioux in the late nineteenth century.

The Ghost Dance simply no longer commands a mass following, having lost its deeper significance and purpose, and it's doubtful anyone now believes in the magical properties once attributed to Ghost Shirts.

Yet, as we've seen, the Ghost Dance arose as a powerful cultural force and revivalist movement in the 1870s and again in the 1890s when it assumed an even stronger – and ultimately more tragic – form.

The Ghost Dance offered a comforting and culture-justifying, religious expression which was both nativistic and revivalistic in content. It provided a utopian vision in response to overwhelmingly desperate conditions facing the Plains Indians.

Those conditions, from the disappearance of the primary food source buffalo; to the loss of lands; to the forced regulations and military domination inflicted on the Indians, all provided a set of problems that were beyond human control, thus opening the way for supernatural solutions offered through a new religion preached by a new prophet.

We've gained further insight into the Ghost Dance by exploring the existence of somewhat similar aboriginal responses to despair and oppression in other parts of the world.

And we've examined some of the potential psychological and spiritual aspects of the Ghost Dance movement .

From all of this analysis, the Ghost Dance has emerged as a less surprising and unusual phenomenon than it may at first have appeared.

Indeed, based on all of the evidence cited, this paper has shown that the Ghost Dance was an understandable, if somewhat radical, response to severe problems that defied anything less than a supernatural solution.

Chapter Two

FROM EXPERTS
TO OBSTACLES:

THE IMPACT OF THE 1660-1870 FUR TRADE ERA ON ABORIGINAL POWER CULTURE, AND INDEPENDENCE

For many Canadians, the image of today's Indians is that of small groups of impoverished people living marginal, welfare-dependent lives in sub-standard housing while contending with community problems ranging from alcoholism to suicides and violence.

Although there are some happy exceptions, the disturbing, pathetic image just described unfortunately holds true for many aboriginal people in Canada.

Yet, fur-trading Indians once enjoyed a far richer and independent life than the modern image or distorted Hollywood Western stereotypes of the past would suggest.

To a significant degree, the extent to which Euro-Canadians depended on Indians, for survival, furs or food and provisions, strongly influenced the degree to which Indians were valued in the emerging Canadian society and the extent to which their personal freedoms, culture and autonomy could be sustained.

The fur trade had a profound impact on the independence of Indians and their ability to be masters of their own destiny.

This chapter will argue that in sharp contrast to dispossessed east coastal Indians, those Indians engaged in the fur trade were accorded a far higher status and effective recognition of autonomy by white society due to the dependence of Euro-Canadian fur traders on Indians to trap and supply furs, and provisions.

I will show that as fur trade competition intensified, the value placed on Indians by fur traders increased, as did the ability of Indians to trade on terms favourable to them while living lives relatively free of Euro-Canadian domination.

Although Indian culture and independence came under pressure to conform to Euro-Canadian values, I will argue that Indians in the fur trade were able to use the commercial value accorded them to retain much of their independence.

Indians were also able to use the fur trade to escape encapsulation by the encroaching white society until the fur trade went into decline towards the end of the 1860s.

I will also examine the ways in which Indians, after the fur trade decline, came to be recast as unwanted obstacles to westward expansionism.

We'll also look at the roles disease, colonization and government intervention played in diminishing the once proud and independent status of the Indians.

Illustrating the plight of all too many Indians, Alice Kehoe suggests that from the mid-1640s, European settlers, along the east coast of what is today the United States, openly disdained Indian agricultural techniques, placed little or no value on Indian land-use culture and made concerted efforts to dispossess the Indians of their land for the purposes of colonization.   1.

> As Kehoe observed:
> "...the Dutch and the succeeding English colonial governments felt little compunction in dispossessing coastal Algonkians, who were only an impediment to colonization and whose principal value lay in what they could bring sold as slaves or, later, hired at wages less than what European settlers would accept."   2.

In sharp contrast, Indians involved in the fur trade were highly regarded as expert woodsmen, guides, provisioners and trappers, not as obstacles to settlement patterns which had yet to make themselves felt in the mid-1600s in the more remote fur-trading areas of North America.

As long as the fur trade remained vibrant in a given geographical area, Indian trappers and middle-men, between trappers and traders, were able to enjoy a co-operative relationship with Euro-Canadians that was largely non-threatening to their culture and independence.

Arthur Ray suggests the degree of control and influence exercised by Indians in the fur trade is yet to be fully appreciated:

> "Students of Indian history need to abandon the assumption that the Indians were ruthless exploited and cheated in all areas by White traders...We must not forget that the Indians became involved in the fur trade by their own choice." 3.

As Ray further observes:

> "The fur trade was a molding force in the economic, political and social development of Canada, and the Indian peoples played a central role in this enterprise." 4.

Bruce Trigger offers further insight into the powerful position of Indians in the fur trade, noting that fur traders were forced to adapt to "not only to native customs but also to a network of political and economic relationships that was not of their own making." 5.

Trigger adds this illustrative commentary:

> "Traders and missionaries alike often were forced to treat Algonkians and Iroquoians as their equals and sometimes they had to acknowledge that the Indians had the upper hand." 6.

Ray further emphasizes the degree of control and influence Indians held over certain aspects of the fur trade, including such key areas as: forcing the traders to adapt to the Indians' barter system through the development of a new barter-monetary device, the 'Made Beaver' exchange system.

As well, Ray cites the ability of Indians to hold the traders to within tight limitations regarding price hikes or reductions in the amount of merchandise being traded for furs as Indians were sharp consumers who could, and would, take their business to rival traders.

Finally, Ray cites the Indians' ability to demand – and receive – abundant gifts of tobacco and other goods before they would even consider trading. 7.

To cite a further example of the measure of Indian power over the fur trade, the Cree south of Hudson Bay were astute businessmen who did little or no trapping themselves.

Instead, the Cree acted as middlemen, trading furs trapped by other tribes for European goods, then retrading these goods to other Indians at substantial mark-ups.

This provided the Cree with a very healthy return for their efforts.

The Cree used their position of military dominance and their trading skills to restrict access to fur traders by other Indians, thus regulating and controlling important trade routes.   8.

This degree of control by the Cree had profound implications. As Ray notes:

"Being in such a position, they were able to dictate the terms of trade to the Europeans and other Indians alike. Furthermore, because of the nature of the system which evolved, they largely regulated the rate of material culture change, and, to a considerable extent, they also influenced its directions."
9.

Indian trappers were so valuable to traders that in times of hardship, the Indians could expect to be fed by the trading post for extended periods of time and advanced trapping equipment on credit.

Peter C. Newman observes that while this placed the Indians in the debt of the Hudson's Bay Company, it had the side benefit of enhancing the care and concern demonstrated for Indians.

As Newman explains:

"The debt load did give them a certain measure of power over the traders: the hunter who starved to death was the worst credit risk

- so the HBC became committed to his welfare." 10.

In the trading process itself, Indians acquired the advantages of Euro-Canadian hunting rifles, kettles and blankets.

However, as Newman notes, "the transfer of technology was not all one-sided."

Newman points out that the Indians:
"...taught the early trader how to harvest wild rice, make clothes from deer or caribou hides and how to put up pemmican, a mixture of died meat, fat and berries that, pounded and packed into ninety-pound bags, became the staple food of the inland fur trade." 11.

The traders heavily depended on the Indians, to provide birch bark canoes for travel; to provide moccasins, snow-shoes and toboggans for winter movement.

Traders also needed the Indians to instruct them in the growing of corn, beans, pumpkins, and squash; to gather wild berries; to teach them how to make maple syrup; to provide tiny settlements with a steady supply of food; and to guide Euro-Canadians through the bush unharmed. 12.

Indeed, the co-operation of Indians was needed not only for the fur trade and for the sustaining of Euro-Canadian settlements, it was also essential in ensuring the opening up of Canadian West.

This important role gave Indians in the fur trade an enhanced status that was denied to Indians further south who were viewed with hostility for standing in the way of colonization.

In described the magnitude of the role played by fur-trading Indians, Hugh Brody asserts:

"Without their co-operation, the early days of Canadian economic development would have been impossible. Despite the dependency that fur traders had to establish among hunters... the place of trappers in the economy as a whole gave them a real importance and, without doubt, a certain dignity." 13.

In the eyes of Euro-Canadians, the sense of dignity, value and respected status they accorded fur-trapping Indians was in many ways a function of their dependency on Indians.

The hunting ability, trapping expertise and survival skills of Indians were held in high regard by

Euro-Canadians who depended on them for their own survival and prosperity.

This in turn gave the Indians involved an enhanced status and ability to exert their own influence in the trade.

Yet, take away this degree of dependency and recast the Indian in the role of one who is trying to save hunting lands from encroaching white society farms and a strikingly different stereotype emerges.

Brody remarks on just such a phenomenon when he contrasts:

> "the smiling, innocent Eskimo; the savage cunning Indian. The one at war with nature, the other with settlers." 14.

As Brody adds:

> "The Eskimo smiles from the sidelines; the 'Indian' is cunning, warlike and stands in our way. This distinction between the two peoples is a geographical and anthropological myth, but the double northern stereotype has none the less persisted." 15.

For as long as they were depended on in the fur trade, Indians enjoyed a relatively high status, to the extent that racial prejudices were remarkably suppressed.

Even mixed marriages, initially banned by the Hudson's Bay Company, became common after the HBC recognized the trading value of forming ties with important tribes.

Sylvia Van Kirk notes that a decades-long ban on European women in the rugged West resulted in traders forming lasting marriages with Indian women in which the women not only provided the benefits of wife and mother but also acted as an interpreter of Indian languages. [16.]

These 'marriages of the country' also provided the trader with important kinship ties to powerful tribes under whose influence much of the fur trade fell and the Indian wives were able to use their position as 'women-in-between' white men and Indian men to their advantage.

The ability of Indian women to act as interpreters and diplomats – offering valued intelligence on the plans of hostile tribes and patching up troublesome trading post-trapper misunderstandings that could have turned violent – enabled the women to achieve recognition and societal influence. [17.]

With other attributes including the ability to make snow-shoes, pitch camps, catch and prepare fish and run a household, Indian women had little difficulty finding white husbands and gaining entry into a fur trade society that offered a less arduous life and featured abundant European goods for themselves and their Indian kin. 18.

With Indian men camping outside the trading posts as a protective home guard against hostile tribes and with Indian women taking part in inter-marriages with white traders, Indians were clearly an integral part of a fur trade society based on mutual dependence between traders and Indians.

It was, without question, a mutually beneficial relationship.

As Robin Fisher observes:
"Certainly the Indians involved in the trade became dependent on the company for European goods, but no more than the Company was dependent on the Indians for furs. Some forts even had to rely on the Indians for their very sustenance, and were therefore doubly dependent. Indians who relied on

provisions took every good advantage of their position..." 19.

Elaborating on this advantageous, mutually-beneficial relationship, Fisher adds:

> "Like Europeans, Indians became fur traders because they perceived that there were benefits to be gained....the Indian and the trader shared certain interests, and the best evidence that both recognized them is the relative lack of hostility between the two groups... The nature of the fur traders' relationship with the Indians restrained any desire for wholesale extermination. Unlike other frontier situations, the fur trade placed no premium on dead Indians." 20.

Fisher also notes that the Hudson's Bay Company restrained from any measures which could have the effect of disrupting Indian trapping.

He adds that Indians were largely able to pick and choose which aspects of Euro-Canadian culture and technology they wished to adopt while efforts by HBC to exert control over them were lacklustre at best. 21.

As Fisher concludes:

"Clearly the fur trade brought change to Indian society, and yet it was change the Indians directed and therefore their culture remained intact. New wealth was injected into Indian culture but not in a way that was socially disruptive, so the cultures were altered but not destroyed. Fur traders occasionally contemplated modifications of Indian customs, but they lacked the power and ultimately the will to effect such changes." 22.

Fisher's somewhat-optimistic observations held true to a significant degree for those Indians who moved west with the fur trade and were able to take advantage of the intense rivalry between the Hudson's Bay Company and the North West Company.

In doing so, the Indians were successfully playing the HBC and Nor' Westers off of each other to extract the most generous gifts and the best Made Beaver returns for their furs.

However, there were hidden costs to be paid by those the fur trade left behind and by those generations of Indians caught with inadequate skills when the fur trade went into steep decline.

Some of those costs first came to light in the Northeast where the fur trade began.

Kehoe notes the previously self-sufficient

and independent Indians of the Northeast had abandoned fishing and hunting skills to take part in the fur trade.

Over the course of generations, the Indians became very dependent on this commercial activity even as it went into decline in the east. Commenting on this plight, Kehoe observes:

> "By the mid-seventeenth century, the Indians of the Northeast were so deeply involved in the fur trade that they were moving into the status of a proletariat. They relied on European manufactures for their daily needs, in many instances having lost their own technologies in stone implements, weapons, and pottery. Metal knives, axes, chisels, awls, needles, and kettles, guns and woollen cloth seemed so cheap compared with the labour needed to make the native analogs that obsolete skills died with the elders." 23.

With strong demand in Europe for furs and with stiff competition between trading companies for greater quantities of fur to meet that demand, the Northeast eventually suffered a depletion of fur-bearing animals.

This depletion prompted the trade to move westward, taking with it Indians who would then establish new lives in less familiar territory, while leaving behind others who were left to cope with a severe drop in their standard of living and a great deal of dependency on European goods.

The Algonquians on the Atlantic coast lost fishing and hunting skills after prolonged involvement in the fur trade and this resulted in a pronounced dependency on less-nutritious European food stuffs and a loss of their prior self-sufficiency.   24.

The depletion of furs, displacement of people and skills and economic boom and bust of the fur trade all formed part of a pattern which was repeated as the trade moved west into new territory.

Kehoe offers this description of the events that unfolded:

> "The fur-trade 'front' advanced westward throughout the eighteenth and nineteenth centuries, leaving behind lands with almost no beaver and few moose, where Indians were forced to subsist on rabbits and fish, rounded out with flour-and-lard bannock biscuit baked from trade provisions, a poor diet that lowered resistance to disease."
> 25.

It became an unfortunate fact of life that as furs began to lose favour as a fashion item in Europe, the affluent days of the fur trade in various parts of Canada were too often followed by an economic decline.

As Kehoe notes:

"From the later seventeenth century in
the Maritimes through the nineteenth century
in western Canada, Indians found that the
heady affluence of first engagement directly
with the European traders (following some
years of receiving goods second-hand from
Indian middlemen) lasted only a generation or
so, and left the sour taste of poverty."
26.

The influence and status of Indians as a valuable asset to traders was also severely diminished with
the merger in 1821 of the Hudson's Bay Company
and North West Company into an expanded Hudson's
Bay Company.

Although the HBC was still faced with much
lesser competitors, the merger meant the end of a
bitter rivalry and effectively brought to a close the
ability of Indians to use the threat of doing business
with a rival trader to command generous gifts and
trading conditions that were highly favourable to
them.   27.

HBC Governor George Simpson quickly took
advantage of his company's enhanced position to
unilaterally impose new arrangements which served to

diminish the Indians position.

For example, the governor substantially reduced the amount of credit that could be extended to
the Indians and the gift giving was cut back from
generous quantities of blankets, tobacco, sugar and
imported teas to consist of a much smaller gift of
some food stuffs.

As well, the quality of goods traded was
diminished after the governor ordered that more
cheaply-made blankets should be traded with the
Indians.

The governor also imposed partial and then
complete bans on Indian access to alcohol – although
these latter measures were actually helpful as many
Indians were becoming addicted.   28.

Simpson also dictated the terms of the fur
trade, imposing a ban on buying furs of animals
trapped in the summer months, barring the use of steel
traps as a conservation measure, and ordering the
temporary stoppage of trapping of certain species of
animals.

He also succeeded in relocating Indians from
one post to another by shutting down numerous posts
that were no longer needed in the absence of strong
competition.

All of these measures imposed new regulations and controls on the Indians. 29.

Faced with shrinking opportunities in the fur trade, many Indians turned from trapping and middle-man roles to instead hunt buffalo and act as food provisioners for trading posts.

However, the intermarriages of the fur trade had created a fast-growing population of racially-mixed Metis who soon gained the upper hand in providing meat to the posts while the fur trade was in steady decline.

As Ray notes:
"Indeed, the deterioration of the competitive position of the Indian in the provision market was further aggravated by the lower volume of demand which was being generated by the fur trade in the 1820s and 1830s. This decline was the result of the reduced scale of operations after 1821, the associated reductions in manpower, the shorter supply routes, and also Simpson's economy measures." 30.

The Metis undermined the position of the Indians in other ways as well.

As Van Kirk suggests, the western-educated

Metis women, with features and manners closer to European notions of beauty and refinement, began to supplant Indian women as preferred brides.

Over time, this placed Metis women in the influential positions of wives of high-ranking settlement officials.   31.

During the 1830s-1840s, the growing presence of white women at the slowly-expanding fur trade settlements worked to supplant both Metis women and Indian women in the upper echelons of frontier society.

Many Indian women became the target of racial put-downs. As Van Kirk observes:
> "In various parts of the British Empire, a direct relationship can be traced between the growth of racial prejudice and the arrival of white women on the scene. With the appearance of women of their own race, some of the fur traders began to exhibit prejudices towards native females which had previously been dormant."   32.

The declining fur trade era finally came to a close around 1870 with the collapse of the fur market, taking a devastating economic toll on Indians who had lost once-valued skills and were now left with skills that were no longer wanted.

Plains Indians were hit especially hard by the fur trade decline as their numbers had been severely diminished due to small pox and other European diseases against which they had little resistance.

Added to these substantial concerns was a sharp decline of the bison, the major source of meat provisions.

By the 1880s, much of the bison herds had been wiped out, with catastrophic consequences.

As Alan McMillan points out:
"The destruction of the bison herds struck at the very lifeblood of the Plains cultures. Wanton slaughter by non-Indians for meat, hides and sport, plus the huge hunts organized by the Metis, left few animals for the competing Plains tribes. The prairies were systematically cleared for European settlement and agriculture. The final disappearance of the herds by the early 1880s was the death knell for the traditional cultures of the Plains nomads." 33.

While the destitute and, in many cases, starving Indians struggled to survive as a people in 1880s, they also found themselves getting in the way of agrarian settlement of West.

The West was being opened up for settlement

by White Canadians thanks to the establishment of the Canadian Pacific Railway and its ability to move in immigrants and take out wheat.

Commenting on the rapid pace of change, James Frideres says it is remarkable just how suddenly economic dominance passed from the Hudson's Bay Company to the CPR.

> As Frideres notes:
> "Within ten years, the West had passed from the influence of a company whose primary concern was the fur trade to that of a company whose major interests centred on settlement and development." 34.

In short order, Indians quickly found themselves being made wards of the state – and the state wasted little time in relocating them to reservations while their former hunting lands became the sites of farms or townships.

It was under these extreme conditions of duress that Indians signed treaties and succumbed to a seemingly never ending series of relocations, disruptions, regulations and accommodations imposed by a White society that now consider them a nuisance.

> As Geoffrey York notes:
> "When the Indian chiefs of the Canadian Prairies signed their treaties in the 1870s,

they were starving and demoralized. Their way of life was already disappearing under the pressures of white settlement, disease, and alcohol." 35.

York further observes that there has been a constant struggle ever since the 1880s by Indians to regain a measure of their lost independence, including their opposition to the 1969 White Paper attempt to eliminate Indian rights and more recent battles to have the right to self government and self-determination clearly recognized in practical terms in the Canadian Constitution. 36.

Today's struggles are all the more poignant when placed in the historical context of the fur trade era: In the space of just a few generations, entire nations of Indian people have gone from independence to extreme dependency.

And they now want, understandably, to regain at least a measure of the control and sense of self determination that past generations had enjoyed.

Throughout this chapter, we've examined the ways in which the fur trade initially helped many Indians escape the racial intolerance, land thefts and degradation non-participants in the trade had been subjected to.

We've also explored the higher status and value

given to fur-trading Indians who were relied upon and respected as expert woodsmen whose prowess at guiding, making snow-shoes and obtaining food from a harsh environment often meant the difference between life and death for the dependent Euro-Canadian traders.

The considerable degree of power and influence held by Indians in the fur trade has been shown to have taken many forms, including: the ability to wrest generous gifts from traders before trade could even begin; the ability to play rival trading companies off of each other to command the highest possible returns for furs traded; the winning of credit and accommodations during lean seasons; the regulating and control of trade by Cree middlemen; the lack of hostilities between traders and Indians; and the ability of Indians to virtually dictate the terms and direction of trade.

This chapter has also illustrated still other ways in which the Indians obtained power and influence during the trade, including the kinship ties, social status and privileges gained through inter-racial marriages with traders.

We've explored the Indians' ability to retain control of hunting and fishing lands and choose which aspects of European technology and culture would be adopted.

Yet, we've also examined how much of this enhanced status, power and influence largely flowed from economic and societal circumstances rather than from any genuine acceptance of Indians as equals or people with legitimate claims to established land uses.

This chapter has shown that the Indians lost much of their trade-enhanced status and influence as soon as the trade became less competitive, then again as it went into decline.

The value accorded them by white society diminished as their trapping prowess, survival skills, land knowledge and expertise in fashioning everything from canoes to snow-shoes and clothing were no longer needed by Euro-Canadians.

We've looked at how the arrival of Metis and then white women prompted a resurgence of previously-suppressed racial prejudices: Once highly-valued Indian-trapper marriages – with all the Indian kinship alliances they involved – eventually became a source of embarrassment and racial slurs within white society.

In the raw Canadian frontier, the Indians had been welcomed as the ideal experts to help the traders fully exploit the initially-lucrative fur market.

In this early context , the Indians were accorded considerable respect, their abilities held in high regard and their women very much appreciated by traders in an otherwise womanless wilderness.

But when the fur trade declined, the Indian experts were no longer needed and they rapidly came to be perceived by white society as obstacles standing in the way of settlement of the Canadian prairies.

The Indians' slide from experts to obstacles was both sudden and steep, taking with it much of their former independence and ability to determine their own future.

To examine this bitter legacy of power held and lost is to gain a fuller understanding and appreciation of the forces shaping today's struggle by aboriginal peoples for self-determination.

Chapter Two
End Notes:

1.   Alice B. Kehoe, North American Indians. A
      Comprehensive Account, (Englewood Cliffs,
      N. J. : Prentice Hall, 1981), pp. 250-252.

2.   IBID, p. 258.

3.   Arthur J. Ray, 'Fur Trade History,' from
      One Century Later: Western Canadian
      Reserve Indians since Treaty 7, (Vancouver:
      University of British Columbia Press, 1978).
4.   IBID.

5. Bruce G. Trigger, 'The French Presence in Huronia: The Structure of Franco-Huron Relations in the First Half of the Seventeenth Century,' from Readings in Canadian History, Pre Confederation, edited by R. Douglas Francis and Donald B. Smith, (Toronto: Holt, Rinehart and Winston of Canada, Ltd., 1990), p. 17.

6. IBID.

7. Arthur J. Ray, Indians In The Fur Trade, (Toronto: University of Toronto Press, 1974), pp. 61-69.

8. IBID, pp. 69-79.

9. IBID, p. 70.

10. Peter C. Newman, Company of Adventurers, (Markham: Penguin Books Canada Ltd., 1985), p. 200.

11. IBID, p. 191.

12. R. Douglas Francis/Richard Jones/ Donald Smith, Origins. Canadian History To Confederation, (Toronto: Holt, Rinehart and Winston of Canada, Ltd., 1988), p. 47.

13. Hugh Brody, Living Arctic. Hunters of the Canadian North, (Vancouver: Douglas & McIntyre Ltd., 1987), p. 201.

14. IBID, p. 21.

15. IBID, p. 20.

16. Sylvia Van Kirk, 'Many Tender Ties'. Women in Fur-Trade Society, 1670-1870, (Winnipeg: Watson and Dwyer Publishing Ltd., 1980), pp. 3-8.

17. IBID, pp. 28-36.

18. IBID, pp. 52-61.

19. Robin Fisher, 'The Land-Based Fur Trade', from Change and Continuity, edited by Carol Wilton, (Toronto: McGraw-Hill Ryerson Ltd., 1992), p. 227.

20. IBID, p. 228.

21. IBID, pp. 229-236.

22. IBID, pp. 235.

23. Alice B. Kehoe, North American Indians, (Englewood Cliffs, N.J.: Prentice Hall, 1981), p. 255.

24.   R. Douglas Francis/ Richard Jones/ Donald Smith, Origins, Canadian History To Confederation, (Toronto: Holt, Rinehart and Winston of Canada Ltd., 1988), p. 42.

25.   Alice B. Kehoe, North American Indians, (Englewood Cliffs: Prentice Hall, 1981), p. 256.

26.   IBID, p. 257.

27.   Arthur J. Ray, Indians In The Fur Trade, (Toronto: University of Toronto Press, 1974), p. 195-196.

28.   IBID, p. 196-199.

29.   IBID, p. 204-210.

30.   Arthur J. Ray, Indians In The Fur Trade, (Toronto: University of Toronto Press, 1974), pp. 206-207.

31.   Sylvia Van Kirk, 'Many Tender Ties', (Winnipeg: Watson and Dwyer Publishing Ltd., 1980), pp. 103-115.

32.   IBID, p. 201.

33. Alan D. McMillan, Native Peoples and Cultures of Canada, (Vancouver: Douglas & McIntyre, 1988), p. 144.

34. James S. Frideres, Native People In Canada. Contemporary Conflicts, 3rd Edition, p. 73.

35. Geoffrey York, The Dispossessed. Life and Death in Native Canada, (Toronto: Lester & Orpen Dennys Publishers, 1989), p. 262.

36. IBID, pp. 250-264.

"…Very good… well written, organized…
a quite objective review."

- McMaster University Anthropology
Professor Victor Gulewitsch commenting
on a book review by Michael B. Davie of Hugh
Brody's Maps And Dreams.

Chapter 3

Reviewing Hugh Brody's
Maps And Dreams

Review: Maps and Dreams, Hugh Brody, Penguin
Books, Markham, 1981

"If the bush ceases to be a place into which
Indians can withdraw, and whose resources they can
rely upon, then they have lost their economy and are
exposed forever to the stereotype that portrays them as
impoverished." (1981: 255)

With this simple, forceful phrase, Maps and
Dreams author Hugh Brody has described the im-
mense importance of the land to the Beaver Indians as
the come into conflict with the disruptive forces of big

business. big government and big game sportsmen.

More importantly, Brody has given a deliberately forgotten people an eloquent voice as the struggle against the designs of oil companies that want to exploit the natural resources and recreational hunters who want to cut into the populations of still-plentiful game.

As Brody notes, it's a very lop-sided conflict between giant energy companies and business-friendly, sympathetic, development-hungry governments versus a total population of no more than 3,500 Indians in northeast British Columbia, including non-status and off-reserve Indians.

Brody, an Oxford University-educated anthropologist and author of several books on aboriginal peoples, strips away the mythology surrounding the Beaver people of Canada's sub-Arctic.

His observations are based on many months of studying and living with the Beaver.

He describes a people pushed back to the northern-most reaches of BC, a people who still hunt and gather for much of their sustenance, make much of their own clothing, expertly trap and fish, practice resource conservation and organize their lives in an efficient, though seemingly haphazard, way.

Brody spent more than a year immersed in the

Beaver culture, hunting with the men, taking part in their activities, carefully watching their interaction with members of White society and keeping the meticulous records of an expert participant-observer.

Through all of this, Brody has genuinely strived to present the developing conflict as it is seen through the eyes of the Beaver people.

Much of the book centres on the views of the Beaver and their interpretation of the events unfolding around them.

Although Maps And Dreams is weighted heavily with the Beavers' point of view, this observation is no more than mild criticism.

Certainly, the other side's point of view has been well-presented elsewhere.

Brody is giving us the opportunity to hear voices previously unheard.

As well, Brody succeeds in injecting a measure of balanced observation through alternating chapters in this book in which native-government history, policies, treaties and practices are clearly laid out before the reader.

After taking the reader through the broken and violated trapping and land use treaties and practices of the past, Brody always returns in the following chapter to the plight of the modern-day Beaver.

As Brody makes clear, the Beaver can only watch helplessly as governments and business contemplate further scarring Beaver lands with roadways or ponder the building of a massive pipeline through the heart of their hunting territory.

"Insofar as there is a conflict of interest in the area," Brody notes, "it is between this small group of people (the Beaver) and an energy frontier whose economic advantages are, to say the least, questionable." (pg. 282)

On reading through Brody's selection of government directives from the distant – and occasionally near – past, it becomes painfully clear that a succession of government officials have exhibited profound ignorance of the Beaver people they sought to "civilize."

The consistent government assumption was that the Beaver were a dying people – who just happened to be taking thousands of years to die out.

"Again and again people have said that one or another Indian society was dead or dying – only to discover, sometimes fifty years later, that it was still alive," Brody observes. "Indians in northeast British Columbia have shown just how resilient a society can be." (pg. 283)

Brody has attempted to bridge this enormous gulf of misunderstanding by bringing the beaver's position to the government in a form it can understand: Much of his book, in fact, surrounds Brody's efforts to get the Beaver to draw their hunting patterns on geographic maps of the region they live in.

These maps are then used to establish land use and support Beaver claims to occupancy.

This is Brody's practical way of avoiding concepts the government would have a much harder time relating to, concepts such as: the Beaver's spiritual connection to the land, their dreams of successful hunts that are made into a happy reality by a form of sympathetic magic, their belief that no person owns the land but the land owns the people who belong to it.

Brody also notes that the Beaver are often reluctant to assert themselves and set the record straight on the way they live.

In one revealing anecdote, Brody describes a casual meeting between a group of Beaver hunters and some White ranchers.

Although the ranchers wrongly assume the Beaver no longer make moccasins and only travel in pickup trucks, the Beaver tribesmen say nothing to correct them.

>As Brody notes:
>"But the Indians did not explain or contradict. They did not even tease back. They simply laughed along with the jokes." (pg. 185)

Brody observes the Beaver's preference to avoid contact with mainstream society, save occasional visits to a nearby town, is a factor in keeping the Indians hidden from those who might attempt to understand them.

But through a collection of richly detailed, well-written anecdotes, Brody takes us inside their fascinating lives.

Brody doesn't ignore any painful moments – drunken, violent parties and on-reserve crime – but these are presented in the much wider context of a struggling yet resourceful people who, though largely self-sufficient and peaceful – are not without internal problems of their own.

Although Brody's probing view of Indian life is remarkable in its intensity and complexity, the Indian voice he brings forward is almost exclusively male.

Despite some passing references to a woman chief and a group of women visiting the town, Brody concentrates heavily on describing his times with the men.

There is, unfortunately, comparatively less effort spent on examining the female perspective.

This again, however, is a relatively minor criticism since Maps And Dreams truly explores uncharted territory through its intimate portrayals of life on a northern BC reserve during times of great change.

Much of the strength of Maps And Dreams is owed to Brody's writing ability.

Through carefully crafted anecdotes and

descriptive passages, Brody takes us deep into the sub Arctic, across mountainous terrain and tundra, through bush and depressing villages of government-built shacks, and into the lives of the Beaver people.

Brody concisely outlines the politics surrounding the Beaver land claims.

He also examines government policy and explains hundreds of years of history in ways that give added meaning to the central theme of Maps And Dreams without in any way detracting from the reader's journey into a unique and hidden society.

As well, Brody has made every effort to use the statements of the Beaver to illustrate their cause in this widely acclaimed, first-rate book.

An example of this can be found when Brody describes a chance meeting between a White hunter and Beaver elder Joseph Patsah, a central figure throughout the book.

When the hunter asks where he should try his luck, Patsah is quick to answer:
> "West. All there to the west. Deer, moose, chickens, cattle, pigs, everything gone to the west. Pretty soon, everything will be gone. All the meat. Then the White man will understand what he has done."
> (pg. 271).

Patsah's resentment over the intrusion of mainstream society becomes more and more understandable, the deeper the reader is drawn into the threatened world of the Beaver.

Brody's attention to detail, his sense of fair play and his effective story-telling ability, combine to give the reader an intimate understanding of a quiet and resilient people.

I highly recommend Brody's Maps And Dreams for anyone interested in gaining a deeper understanding of the plight faced by a marginalized people.

The following chapter offers an examination of a non-North American aboriginal society, the Kaluli. Based on Edward L. Schieffelin's The Sorrow of the Lonely and the Burning of the Dancers

Chapter Four

GISARO

A CEREMONY
OF RECIPROCITY
AND RELEASE
IN KALULI CULTURE

The Gisaro ceremony reveals a great deal about the cultural and societal values of the Kaluli people of the Bosavi region of the great Papuan Plateau on the island of New Guinea.

With its central characteristics of reciprocity and emotional release, Gisaro transcends the limitations of a ceremonial dance to embody the deepest, most personal experiences of the audience.

Gisaro both shapes and is shaped by Kaluli society, providing a reflection of societal norms and a manifestation of the core of Kaluli culture.

This chapter examines these aspects of Gisaro, as presented by Edward L. Schieffelin in his book The Sorrow of the Lonely and the Burning of the Dancers, and explains how Gisaro plays a key role in illustrating and perpetuating the societal value system of the Kaluli.

Gisaro, as with all Kaluli ceremonies, takes place in the main longhouse at night and lasts until dawn.

It serves to forge new relationships among its audience and participants while reaffirming old relationships.

Schieffelin, whose field work included two years - 1966-1968 - among the Kaluli, remarked on the powerful socializing role of Gisaro, observing that Gisaro is the "most elaborate and characteristic ceremony of this type." (Schieffelin 1976: 21).

The sharing and distribution of food is central to Kaluli culture and in this Gisaro often plays a key role in providing a ceremonial, celebratory framework in which food is exchanged in a culturally-sustaining system of reciprocity among the Kaluli whose name, very roughly translated means "the real men".

Gisaro lends a sense of drama and importance to the core value of reciprocity in Kaluli life.

As Schieffelin observes:
"Reciprocity is also bound up with cultural values pertaining to balance and proportion in human relationships and consequently becomes implicated in matters as far afield as sexual desire, moral philosophy, medicine and theatre." (Schieffelin 1976: 2).

How Gisaro works to perpetuate systems of reciprocity and cultural continuity can best be understood with a further, closer examination of this ceremony.

An analysis of Gisaro will serve to illustrate the many ways in which it pervades Kaluli society, reflecting and reinforcing deeply entrenched societal values and beliefs, including an underlying sense of fatalism, a parallel unseen world and a magic-influenced life-force.

There is a slow build-up to Gisaro, a ceremony that can take weeks to prepare.

Drumming fills the longhouse clearing for much of the day until it is announced that the Gisaro dancers are ready.

The dancers move in silence as the hushed crowd prepares for the spectacle ahead.

Abruptly all dancers, save one, sink to the floor in silence.

The lone standing dancer cuts a compelling figure that is at once both awe-inspiring and pathetic.

With his painted face making him unrecognizable - yet eerily familiar - to members of the audience, the dancer bounces and bobs, his plumage of feathers and leaves swaying to the rattle of a shell.

Singing fills the air as longhouse members with torches draw near to illuminate his oddly remote figure (Schieffelin 1976: 172-177).

Schieffelin suggests that the singing dancer appears withdrawn, leaving it to the audience to perhaps "perceive a reflection of themselves," in this dancer who appears "remote, archetypal, a figure emerging from an infinite distance, another time and place." (Schieffelin 1976: 176-177).

The dancer is often not a member of the longhouse community he performs at but is instead an outsider who incorporates local places and names into his songs.

In so doing, he strikes a universal chord among audience members who see in his persona, a nostalgic, sometimes fatalistic return to their past.

Schieffelin notes that the dancers affect on audience members is uniquely intimate to each individual.

He observes that a Kaluli man watching the dancer finds that "in his mask like face he recognizes his dead brother (or other relative,)" and begins to share the suffering and sorrow the dancer feels in his arduous performance (Schieffelin 1976: 177-180).

In our own culture, we can sometimes experience the barest hint of what Schieffelin describes when a song on the radio suddenly strikes a nostalgic, emotional chord, flooding our minds with sensations and memories of the past.

Of Gisaro, Schieffelin observes that "framed in sentiments of loneliness or abandonment, the mention of particular trees, hills, and other details of the locality evoke for the listeners particular times and circumstances." (Schieffelin 1976: 181).

Fatalism is apparent in passages which refer to lost children, settlement ruins and catastrophic storms - all compelling images for Kaluli who believe they are slowly dying out as a people (Schieffelin 1976: 180-181).

The Gisaro experience appears to tap emotions at a far deeper level, awakening in the Kaluli long-suppressed feelings of grief and anguish which are suddenly released (Schieffelin 1976: 180-184).

Gisaro-induced release of grief is often triggered by a song's reference to the death of a member of the host longhouse although even a seemingly obscure reference to a place name can be enough to prompt an cathartic release of emotional pain as diverse members of the audience read their own personal meaning into the song's haunting, locality-based messages.

Repetition lends an abstract quality to the dance while the dancer's detachment from the songs increases the likelihood that the audience will assume a sense of personal ownership of the song and its perceived messages. (Schieffelin 1976: 187-190).

Eventually, as the dancer's song and its accompanying chorus take the audience near places where kin have died, a deep sense of loss and feelings of grief rush to the surface of some audience members and the dancer is burned by torches to pay for his intrusion and for the otherwise embarrassing display of emotion he has provoked.

As Schieffelin notes, "this painful tension between grief, anger, intimacy, and violence becomes visible when someone from the audience angrily thrusts the torch out on the dancer's shoulder and then throws his arms around him, hugging him affectionately and wailing uncontrollably." (Schieffelin 1976: 190).

Schieffelin notes that burning the dancers with torches is not considered a serious injury although it can take weeks for a burn to heal.

He adds that the violence is carefully controlled by many members of the audience and that "the violence of the audience does not disrupt the performance because it is absorbed and contained within it." (Schieffelin 1976: 192).

Although efforts are made to shield the dancers from the worst effects of a direct burning by the torches, no effort is made to actually stop members of the audience from burning the dancer.

The Kaluli feel it would be wrong to deny grieving aa biso (hosts) the right to burn the dancer as payment for making them grieve.

As Schieffelin observes:

"From the Kaluli point of view, the

main object of Gisaro is not the burning of the dancers. On the contrary, the point is for the dancers to make the hosts burst into tears. The hosts then burn the dancers in angry revenge for the suffering they have been made to feel." (Schieffelin 1976: 24).

Indeed, the performers provide the aa biso with gifts in an act of reciprocity to atone for making the hosts cry.

As Schieffelin observes: "A mirror, a box of paint, a small knife, a shell necklace - these soothe the feelings and terminate the anger of the aa biso and establish reassurance of the mutual spirit of closeness between the two sides." (Schieffelin 1976: 194).

The drama of Gisaro, as Schieffelin points out, is that it is an opposition scenario, within a reciprocity structure that resolves tensions with limited, proportional violence within the bounds of a ceremony in which "the listeners' feelings and reactions are not merely a response to the performance; they are integral to its structure and significance." (Schieffelin 1976: 197).

Indeed, an attempt by a local administrative officer to ban the burning of dancers only resulted in a more violent release of pent-up anger by the Gisaro audience with more serious injuries to the dancer (Schieffelin 1976: 204-206).

The elements of reciprocity and violent retribution inherent in Gisaro permeate other aspects of Kaluli culture, including the occasions which Kaluli celebrate with Gisaro.

These events, as Schieffelin recounts, "are nearly always bound up with important transactions of social reciprocity in their relationships with one another." (Schieffelin 1976: 25).

For example, in a wedding ceremony celebrated with Gisaro, a bride and procession are formally brought into the groom's house.

Then, bridewealth is exchanged (an act of recognition and partial compensation to her family for the loss of her productivity), and a ceremony is performed that night.

Similarly, the Kaluli may celebrate an abundance of pigs or crops by collecting them and redistributing both at the hosts' longhouse during ceremonies coupled with Gisaro.

All of this is can be seen as a celebrated manifestation of an exchange system core to Kaluli life, a system in which friends and relatives lend and expect to borrow tools, food and wealth on the basis of need; in which the exchange of women forges alliances; in which gifts of food prompt reciprocal gifts (Schieffelin 1976: 25-26).

Gisaro reflects and partially encompasses the pervasive extent to which culturally-engrained sharing and reciprocity resonate throughout Kaluli society.

As Schieffelin writes:

"Indeed, while celebrating occasions of reciprocity, Gisaro embodies some of its characteristics. Compensation (su) must be paid for feelings deeply moved, and one ceremony is explicitly given in return (wel) for another. A performance that has caused a lot of grief motivates the hosts to return an equally affecting one to their guests. Gisaro is itself, therefore, a reciprocal transaction in the aesthetic domain. All this suggests that social reciprocity is not merely punctuated by ceremonies such as Gisaro but is deeply bound up with what they express. Gisaro clearly involves emotional or ideological matters of wider cultural significance than only the giving of food. It points to ways that reciprocity may be bound up with other realms of cultural symbolism and social experience." (Schieffelin 1976: 27-28).

The impact of Gisaro songs which refer to locality relates to the central importance the Kaluli place on locality as core to identity.

In a sense, where one lives is also who one is. Schieffelin notes that:

"Over a period of time, the community becomes bound up with the area it moves about in and comes to be referred to by the name of the locality. Thus, for example, lineages of Gaesumisi and Wabisi whose communities successive longhouses have been located in the vicinity of Baegolo Ridge are called Baegolo people." (Schieffelin 1976: 41).

Schieffelin notes that locality offers linkages of shared experience between generations. He adds that "Kaluli identify themselves with place names because they see themselves reflected in their lands." (Schieffelin 1976: 45).

Coupled with a close identification with the visible locality connection are societal ties that are also structured to fit a physical reality in which close friends are sometimes recast as brothers through genealogical reckoning which can contradict and take precedence over descent.

This can encompass elements of a clan in which genealogical ties are assumed but not proven.

Closest ties are between members of the immediate family and affines while ties beyond the second ascending generation are often lost.

As well, it is through the exchange of food, not the mere existence or otherwise of blood ties, that relationships are made socially real (Schieffelin 1976: 56-63).

The central role given men in Gisaro can be more readily understood via scrutiny of Kaluli societal norms and values which serve to relegate women to the sidelines of political power.

Commenting on the Kaluli view of women, Schieffelin writes:

> "Menstruating or not, women are considered weakened people, and prolonged intimate contact with them or their things is detrimental to men's health and stamina. This is the primary reason why the women sleep separately from the men in the longhouse. It is also the reason why, when a man marries and comes into close contact with a woman, he must, in effect, take up her taboos and eat only smoked meat." (Schieffelin 1976: 67).

The Kaluli are not alone among New Guinea peoples in their view of women.

M. J. Meggitt notes that Kuman of Chimbu in the New Guinea Highlands regard women as mentally inferior and dangerous, while the Kyaka consider menstruating women to be unclean bearers of pollution and the Mae consider menstruation blood as potentially lethal to men, necessitating various taboo-oriented aversion practices and use of protective magic. (Meggitt 1966: 202-209).

As far-fetched as menstruation taboos against eating certain foods or handling children may appear to Western eyes, for the Kaluli, these practices provide a sense of limited control over one's destiny, along with explanations and a sense of meaning for otherwise difficult to explain ailments.

The Kaluli also make assertive efforts to resolve disputes by forming opposition groups which cross kinship lines and pit one interest group against another to confront a pressing issue, using the aa longhouse as an arena in which arguments can be heard, compensation paid and a system of reciprocity maintained in this essentially egalitarian society (Schieffelin 1976: 92).

To the Kaluli, events in life, including death are by design, not accident.

Schieffelin notes:

> "Every death is caused by a witch (sei). A sei attacks the victim invisibly, but a man who is very sick is sometimes able to perceive him while in the liminal consciousness of high fever. If the patient thinks he is going to die, he will whisper to close kin the identity of the person he thinks he sees. When a person dies he has in effect been murdered. If he was a beloved or important person, his kinsmen are furious, and in response, traditionally, they would organize a raid to kill the sei." (Schieffelin 1976: 78).

Although the practice described above was abandoned in 1966, it continues to provide a clear illustration of the Kaluli system of retaliation and informal justice.

After the sei had been killed with blows from a rock to the head, his heart was removed and if soft to the touch, the murdered man was considered to be a sei.

Even so, the relatives of the murdered man still had to be appeased through gifts of wealth such as axes and pearl shells to compensate them for the loss of his life (Schieffelin 1976: 78-80).

To Western eyes this no doubt appears to be a form of exceptionally rough justice - and it is indeed difficult to make a strong argument of support for what is essentially premeditated murder.

Yet the abandoned practice serves to illustrate the Kaluli way of affixing meaning to a natural occurrence (death), confronting it in a decisive manner and resolving it through retaliation and reciprocity.

Schieffelin writes:
"The Kaluli reaction in confrontation with death and loss is to strike back... through the opposition scenario, life, in its vitality, forced death to pay its due. It was not a happy state of affairs but it had its dignity and the Kaluli lived with it." (Schieffelin 1976: 160).

Death, not surprisingly, also finds expression in that most-central of ceremonies, Gisaro.
To the Kaluli, there is an unseen world inhabited by Kaluli spirits, in which the living and dead can find their counterpart in a bird or insect or pig.

Gisaro plays a central role in resolving grief

over death, giving meaning to death and helping the survivors cope with its aftermath.

Through the Gisaro ceremony, members of the audience are able to fall into a trance like state in which they visit or experience glimpses of the unseen world and communicate with the dead through seance.

As Schieffelin suggests:
"Gisaro not only recalls to Kaluli their sorrows and their dead but establishes a solidarity between them. Singing Gisaro with one's dead brother at a seance is one way, for a short while, of being with him again." (Schieffelin 1976: 213).

Of Gisaro's unique role in providing a bridge to the dead, Schieffelin notes that "it clearly plays an important part on a whole other (though hidden) level of Kaluli experience - in an invisible journey of the dead. There seems to be no clear counterpart to these events in the visible realm..." (Schieffelin 1976: 216).

Of Gisaro's ability to pull various aspects of Kaluli life into a comprehensive form from which meaning can be derived, Schieffelin writes:
"Gisaro put the events of life, death and the passing of time into intelligible relationship without at the same time putting them at a reflective distance. Thus, they may be resolved emotionally and accepted concretely

in committed real action. Gisaro is therefore more than a statement concerning life. It is a thrusting of oneself on it. It is not so much a reflection of death as it is an assertion against it." (Schieffelin 1976: 211-212).

As Schieffelin also notes:

"the ceremony generates, in the abstract, the movement of Kaluli social life itself. For it is the formation of oppositions and the progression towards their resolution, whether over death and dispute or weddings and prestations that provides the motion of social and political events." (Schieffelin 1976: 211).

Gisaro maintains systems of orderly reciprocity and gives vent to antagonisms and emotional outpourings which are then resolved in a formal healing process (Schieffelin 1976: 210).

From all of this, it is evident that Gisaro transcends the usual limitations of ceremony by presenting a means by which suppressed emotions can emerge for needed release, disputes can be confronted and resolved and limited violence can be safely contained.

With its inherent reciprocity, Gisaro is highly representative of Kaluli societal norms and values.

Gisaro also plays a central role in the forging and renewing of kinship ties.

It is the setting for weddings, for passages of rites, for visiting the dead, for reconciling animosities and coping with tragedies.

Gisaro often performs the role of entertainer, commentator and judge.

Members of the audience become part of an individually interpreted personal experience which recasts them from observer to participant.

Gisaro is a cultural phenomena which offers an unusual form of justice - the burning of dancers - that is accepted by the Kaluli as a limited release of tensions which might otherwise find expression in still more violent forms.

Perhaps most importantly, Gisaro exposes and then resolves conflicts.

It instils meaning and a sense of purpose to Kaluli attempts to cope with the loss of loved ones.

It brings the society together by defining and perpetuating shared cultural bonds with each elaborate ceremony.

Gisaro, then, is considerably more than a reflection of Kaluli culture, it is in some instances its very embodiment and is at all times a pervasive and integral part of that culture.

The Gisaro ceremony provides a personalized experience for its observers, conjuring up intimate memories and a renewed connection with the dead.

For Kaluli society as a whole, it addresses the losses of the past and offers each new generation a bridge to the last.

Gisaro is a central cultural experience among the Kaluli and a compelling manifestation of the society's collective memory.

Closing Notes

Perhaps it can be said that one man's superstition and magic is another man's religion.

Indeed, with the exception of the Ghost Shirt, which, unfortunately did not render Indians impervious to bullets, there is much in the aboriginal belief systems we've just studied that could fit in mainstream religions.

The Ghost Dance and Cargo Cults essentially present the practitioners as the chosen people and hold forth promises of a better life ahead. Sound familiar?

This has, I trust, been an interesting and enlightening journey into the cultures and spiritual beliefs of other peoples.

Indeed, Following the Great Spirit has closely examined some of the cultural values and spiritual mindset of North American Indians and other aboriginal peoples in crisis situations and times of great change.

We explored the connection of aboriginal people to the land, to the natural world to ancient rituals and long established traditions.

And we examined their reliance – much like the rest of us – on turning to powers greater than themselves in times of upheaval.

We began with a look at the Ghost Dance, a phenomena that sprang forth when North American Indians were displaced from hunting grounds, dispossessed of lands and in some cases assimilated to accommodate encroaching white settlements in the latter half of the 1800s.

Seeking salvation, the Indians turned to the Ghost Dance, a somewhat-utopian spiritual belief system that helped the dispossessed Cherokee, Sioux, Paiute, Klamath and Plains Indians in the U.S., and

Dakota Indians in Canada, cope with their sudden displacement, alienation and rapidly growing sense of despair.

This spiritual dance promised the return of dead Indians and game in a new age of abundance, with the Indians being very much in control of their collective destiny.

The cargo cults of New Guinea and Melanesia also allowed practitioners to use religious principles to help their followers cope with a crisis that has thwarted their efforts to have a more satisfying culture.

These cults also put the Indians in charge while the White men are eradicated – but leave their possessions (cargo) behind for the Natives to enjoy.

We also explored the rare, exulted status Indians enjoyed through the boom times of the fur trade.

And we found the Indians lost a great deal when the fur trade boom times came to an end.

To get a sense of how badly things can go awry when Indians lose their value in White society, we turned to a review of Hugh Brody's excellent maps And Dreams.

And we explored the Gisaro ceremony and the way it reveals a great deal about the cultural and societal values of the Kaluli people of the Bosavi region of the great Papuan Plateau on the island of New Guinea.

It was for me, as I hope it was for you, a journey well worth taking.

- **Michael B. Davie.**

Bibliography

1. Becker, Ernest, The Birth and Death of Meaning. An Interdisciplinary Perspective on the Problem of Man, New York: The Free Press, McMillan Publishing Co., 1962.

2. Brody, Hugh, Living Arctic. Hunters of the Canadian North, Vancouver: Douglas & McIntyre Ltd., 1987.

3. Brody Hugh, Maps and Dreams, Penguin Books, Markham, 1981.

4. Cummins, Walter M, Green, Martin and Verhulst, Margaret, The Other Sides of Reality, San Francisco: Boyd & Fraser, 1972.

5. Fisher, Robin, 'The Land-Based Fur Trade', from Change and Continuity, edited by Carol Wilton, Toronto: McGraw-Hill Ryerson Ltd., 1992.

6. Francis, R. Douglas, /Richard Jones/ Donald Smith, Origins. Canadian History To Confederation, Toronto: Holt, Rinehart and Winston of Canada, Ltd., 1988.

7. Frideres, James S., Native People In Canada. Contemporary Conflicts, 3rd Edition.

8. Kehoe, Alice B., North American Indians. A Comprehensive Account, Englewood Cliffs, N. J. : Prentice Hall: 1981.

9. Laubin, Reginald, and Laubin, Gladys, Indian Dances of North America, Norman, Oklahoma: University of Oklahoma Press, 1976.

10. Lewis, I. M., Religion In Context. Cults and Charisma, Cambridge, U.K.: Cambridge University Press, 1986.

11. McDonnell, Janet, A., The Dispossession of The American Indian, Indianapolis: Indiana University Press, 1991.

12. McMillan, Alan D., Native Peoples and Cultures of Canada, Vancouver: Douglas & McIntyre, 1988.

13. Meggitt, M. J., 'Male-Female Relationships in the Highlands of Australian New Guinea, American Anthropologist, 1966.

14. Mooney, James, 'The Fourteenth Annual Report of the Bureau of Ethnology,' Washington: Government Printing Office, 1896. Republished in: The Ghost-Dance Religion and The Sioux Outbreak of 1890, Chicago: University of Chicago Press, 1965.

15. Murphy, Robert, F., Cultural & Social Anthropology, An Overture, Englewood Cliffs, N.J.: Prentice Hall, 1979.

16. Newman, Peter C., Company of Adventurers, Markham: Penguin Books Canada Ltd., 1985.

17. Ray, Arthur J. Ray, 'Indians In The Fur Trade', Toronto: University of Toronto Press: 1974.

18. Ray, Arthur J., 'Fur Trade History,' from One Century Later: Western Canadian Reserve Indians since Treaty 7, Vancouver: University of British Columbia Press: 1978.

19. Schieffelin, Edward, L., The Sorrow of the Lonely and the Burning of the Dancers, New York: St. Martin's Press, 1976.

20. Spier, Leslie, The Ghost Dance of 1870 Among The Klamath of Oregon, Seattle: University of Washington Press, 1927.

21. Thornton, Russell, American Indian Holocaust and Survival, Seattle: University of Washington Press, 1927.

22. Trigger, Bruce G., 'The French Presence in Huronia: The Structure of Franco-Huron Relations in the First Half of the Seventeenth Century,' from Readings in Canadian History, Pre Confederation, edited by R. Douglas Francis and Donald B. Smith, Toronto: Holt, Rinehart and Winston of Canada, Ltd: 1990.

23. Van Kirk, Sylvia, 'Many Tender Ties'. Women in Fur-Trade Society, 1670-1870, Winnipeg: Watson and Dwyer Publishing Ltd., 1980.

24. York, Geoffrey, The Dispossessed. Life and Death in Native Canada, Toronto: Lester & Orpen Dennys Publishers, 1989.

25. Wallace, Anthony, F. C., 'Nativism and Revivalism,' from Magic, Witchcraft, and Religion. An Anthropological Study of the Supernatural, edited by Arthur C. Lehmann and James E. Myers, Mountain View, California: Mayfield Publishing Company, 1985.

26. Worsley, Peter, M., 'Cargo Cults,' from Magic, Witchcraft and Religion, Mountain View, California: Mayfield Publishing, 1985.

Manor House Publishing Inc.
(905) 648-2193

Manor House Publishing Inc.
(905) 648-2193

www.ingramcontent.com/pod-product-compliance
Lightning Source LLC
Chambersburg PA
CBHW021835020426
42334CB00014B/646